Plottr

Plan Your Books Like a Pro

The Future of Book Outlining is Already Here

www.plottr.com/future

Leader
SOURCEFORGE
Spring
2023

Capterra ★★★★★ 4.9

Software Suggest
Trending
WINTER
2023

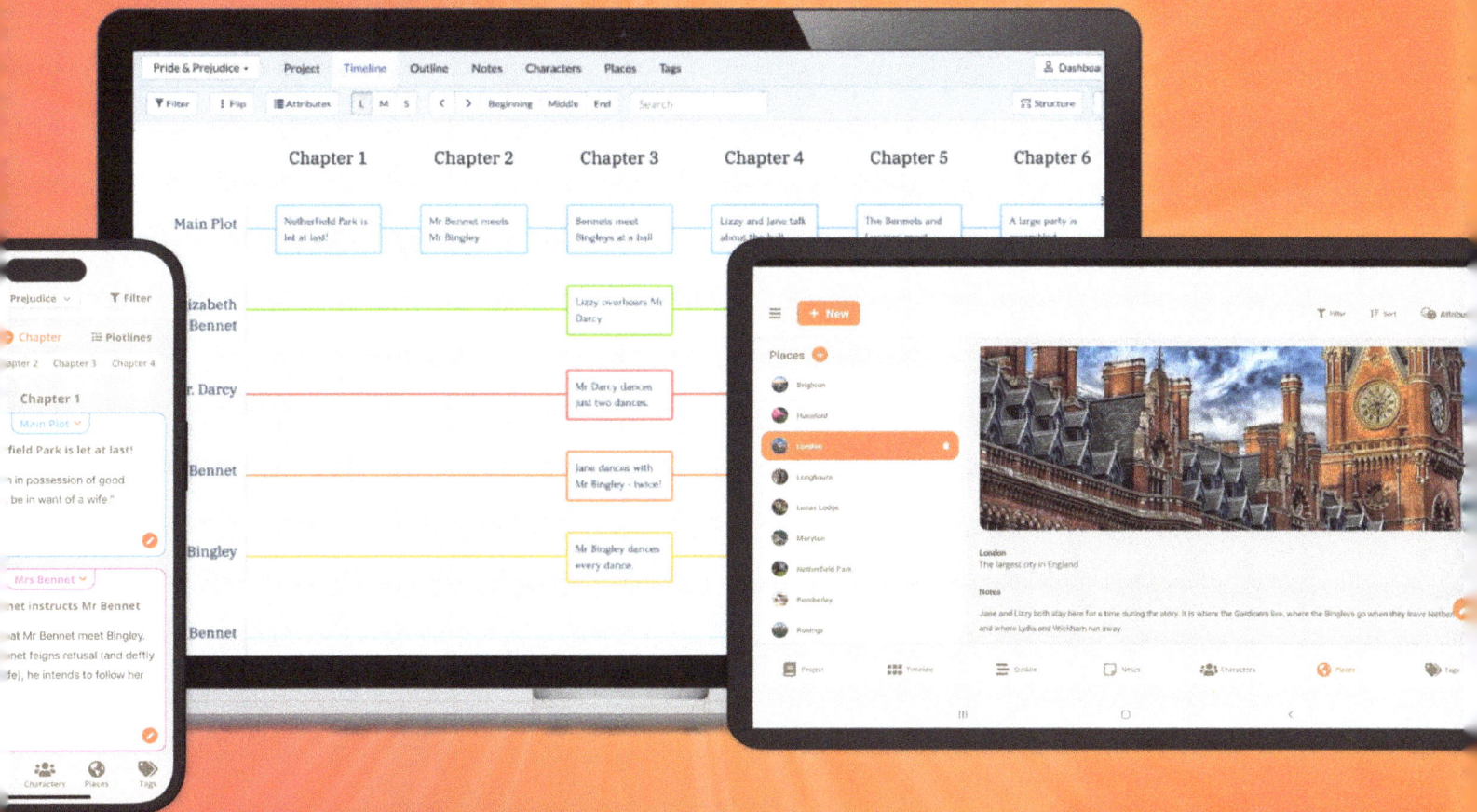

Alliance of Independent Authors

FOR
SELF-PUBLISHING
**NOVELISTS,
POETS** AND
**NON-FICTION
AUTHORS**

Unlock your full potential as an Independent Author

Access the support and resources of the Alliance of Independent Authors

Join the world's only non-profit professional writing organization representing independent authors globally.

Harness a wealth of resources, expertise, and community support, all tailored for you and your books.

- Tools & Resources
- Mentors & Advisors
- Legal & Rights
- Member Support Desk
- Webinars & Workshops
- Vibrant Community
- Discounts & Deals
- Free guidebooks, handbooks and member magazine

PUBLISHING GUIDES FOR INDIE AUTHORS 1

Creative Self-Publishing
ALLi's Guide to Independent Publishing for Authors and Poets

Orna A. Ross

PUBLISHING GUIDES FOR INDIE AUTHORS 2

Choose the Best Self-Publishing Services
ALLi's Guide to Assembling Your Tools and Your Team

John Doppler

PUBLISHING GUIDES FOR INDIE AUTHORS 3

Reach More Readers, Sell More Books
ALLi's Guide to Book Marketing for Authors and Poets

Orna A. Ross

PUBLISHING GUIDES FOR INDIE AUTHORS 4

Your Book in Bookstores
ALLi's Guide to Print Book Distribution for Authors

Debbie P. Young

PUBLISHING GUIDES FOR INDIE AUTHORS 5

150 Self-Publishing Questions Answered
ALLi's Writing, Publishing, & Book Marketing Tips for Authors and Poets

M.L. Ronn

PUBLISHING GUIDES FOR INDIE AUTHORS 6

How Authors License Publishing Rights
ALLi's Guide to Working with Publishers, Producers and Others

Orna A. Ross

Become a member today, visit:
www.allianceindependentauthors.org/join
or Scan the QR code

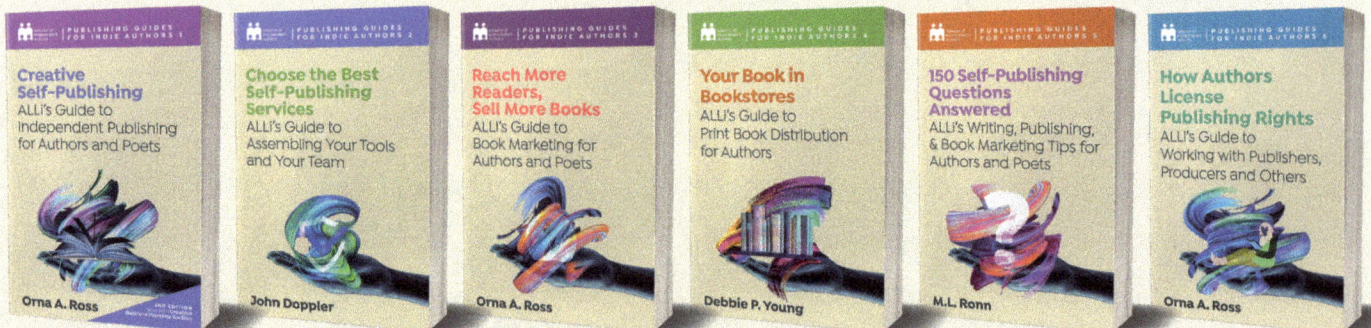

INDIE AUTHOR MAGAZINE

HELLO AND WELCOME!

I'm Indie Annie, and I'm thrilled you're reading this gorgeous full-color version of IAM. Did you know that you can also access all the information, education, and inspiration in our app? It's available on both the iOS App Store and Google Play. And for those that prefer to listen to me read articles, you can pop over to Spotify or our website.

Happy Reading! X

IndieAuthorMagazine.com

Download on the App Store

GET IT ON Google Play

Spotify

STORYTELLER
OPERATING SYSTEM

NOTION FOR AUTHORS

LEARN:

The PARA Method for Writers
Building Your Story Bible
Setting up Books and Series
Task Management for Writing
Task Management for Editing, ARCs, and Betas
Collaborating in Notion
Incorporating Other Apps into Notion
Automating Workflows
And More!

SIGN UP: INDIEAUTHORTRAINING.COM

" I joined while having a crisis with Amazon KDP... The Alliance is a beacon of light. I recommend that all indie authors join...
Susan Marshall

" The Alliance is about standing together.
Joanna Penn

" It's the good stuff, all on one place.
Richard Wright

" "ALLi has helped me in myriad ways: discounts on services, vetting providers, charting a course to sales success. But more than anything it's a community of friendly, knowledgeable, helpful people."
Beth Duke

See hundreds more testimonials at:
AllianceIndependentAuthors.org/testimonials

IAM

TRANSLATIONS

PLANNING TRAVEL TO A CONFERENCE?

Use miles.

Explore ways to make the most of your award miles.

Writelink.to/unitedair

Authorpreneurs in Action

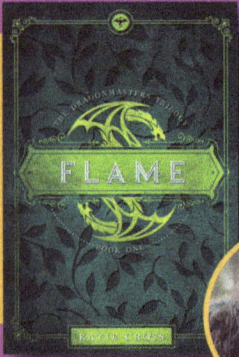

"I love Lulu! They've been a fantastic distributor of my paperbacks and an excellent partner as I dive into direct sales. They integrate so smoothly with my personal Shopify store, and their customer support has been top notch."

Katie Cross, katiecrossbooks.com

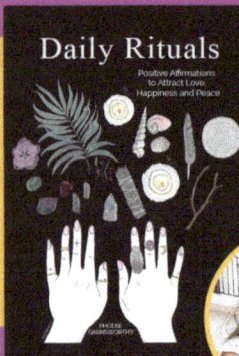

"Having my own store has given me the freedom to look at my creativity as a profitable business and lifelong career."

Phoebe Garnsworthy, phoebegarnsworthy.com

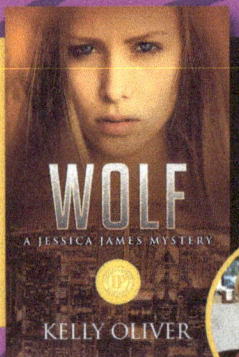

"Lulu has a super handy integration with Shopify. Lulu makes it so easy to sell paperbacks directly to readers."

Kelly Oliver, kellyoliverbooks.com

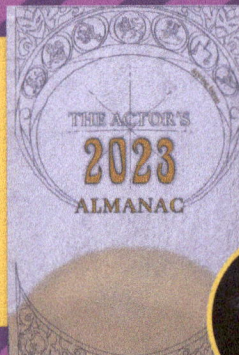

"My experience with Lulu Direct has been more convenient and simple than I anticipated or thought possible. I simply publish, take a step back and allow the well-oiled machine to run itself. Most grateful!"

Molly McGivern, theactorsalmanac.com

lulu*direct*

Sell Smarter, Not Harder.

Sell Books from Your Website Using Lulu Direct

Keep 100% of your profit

Retain customer data

Integrate with Shopify, WooCommerce, Zapier, & Custom API

Get paid quickly

No monthly fees

Fully automated white-label fulfillment

Global print network

B Corp Certified

Dropshipping Multiple Orders for a New Book Launch or Crowdfunding Campaign? Use the Lulu Order Import Tool!

We make dropshipping multiple orders at once easier than ever!

- ✓ Upload your book on Lulu for free
- ✓ Use the Order Import Tool to upload a file with your customer's order and shipping information
- ✓ We'll professionally print the orders and drop ship each one to your fans around the world

Get exclusive Publishing & Marketing tips to help you create and sell your books more effectively!

lulu

@luludotcom   lulu.com

INDIE
AUTHOR MAGAZINE

EDITORIAL

Publisher | Chelle Honiker

Editor in Chief | Nicole Schroeder

Creative Director | Alice Briggs

Partner Relationship Manager | Elaine Bateman

ADVERTISING & MARKETING

Inquiries
Ads@AtheniaCreative.com

Information
Partner.IndieAuthorMagazine.com

CONTRIBUTORS

Angela Archer, Elaine Bateman, Bradley Charbonneau, Jackie Dana, Heather Clement Davis, Jamie Davis, Laurel Decher, Gill Fernley, Jen B. Green, Jac Harmon, Marion Hermannsen, Jenn Lessmann, Megan Linski-Fox, Angie Martin, Merri Maywether, Kevin McLaughlin, Jenn Mitchell, Tanya Nellestein, Susan Odev, Eryka Parker, Tiffany Robinson, Joe Solari, David Viergutz

SUBSCRIPTIONS
https://indieauthormagazine.com/subscribe/

HOW TO READ
https://indieauthormagazine.com/how-to-read/

WHEN WRITING MEANS BUSINESS
IndieAuthorMagazine.com

Athenia Creative | 6820 Apus Dr., Sparks, NV, 89436 USA | 775.298.1925

ISSN 2768-7880 (online)–ISSN 2768-7872 (print)

The publication, authors, and contributors reserve their rights in regards to copyright of their work. No part of this work covered by the copyright may be reproduced or copied in any form or by any means without the written consent of the publisher. All copyrighted work was reproduced with the permission of the owner.

Reasonable care is taken to ensure that *Indie Author Magazine* articles and other information on the website are up to date and as accurate as possible, at the time of publication, but no responsibility can be taken by *Indie Author Magazine* for any errors or omissions contained herein. Furthermore, *Indie Author Magazine* takes no responsibility for any losses, damages, or distress resulting from adherence to any information made available through this publication. The opinions expressed are those of the authors and do not necessarily reflect the views of *Indie Author Magazine*.

THE NEW WAY FOR READERS TO FIND AUTHORS SELLING DIRECT

DIRECT2READERS

A unique directory where you can connect directly with your fans and keep all your hard-earned profits.

💡 Innovative Recommendation Engine: Our natural language recommendation engine helps readers discover books based on their preferences. Say goodbye to clunky categories!

📈 New Market Access: Gain exposure to a new segment of avid readers, all hungry for fresh indie voices.

💵 Zero Commissions: You read it right! We don't take a cut. Your profits are yours to keep.

🚀 Boost Your Sales: Benefit from our advanced marketing and influencer channels designed to supercharge your direct sales.

🌐 **Register Now**
Direct2Readers.com

EDITOR IN CHIEF

Since *Indie Author Magazine*'s inception, we've tried to reflect what we've always believed about building a career as an indie author: that there's no single "right" way to do it. We've always worked to ensure every author can see their journey somewhere within these pages, whether they choose to publish wide or remain exclusive to Amazon, whether they connect with readers on social media or at in-person events, and whether they are just starting their career or have a well-established back list and crowds of adoring readers. We've tried to include as many experiences as we can through the stories of the authors we feature on our covers and by sharing your questions with Indie Annie.

As we celebrate our third year of publication in 2024, we want to share even more author voices with you. Beginning in this issue, we've turned our regular column pages into rotating, multi-part series, to spotlight even more authors' insights on a variety of topics. If you read our magazine regularly, you'll already have seen some messages from Joe Solari, of Author Nation, on creating sustainable business strategies. This month, you'll hear from Megan Haskell about the future of our industry and what opportunities it will create for your career.

Translations, the focus of this month's issue, are all about giving more voices to your story in order to share it with more readers. We hope *IAM* can continue to offer the same for your author story. If you have an article you'd like to see in the magazine or a question to share with Indie Annie, please reach out! Submit ideas for articles you'd like to see at https://indieauthormagazine.com/tell-us-a-story, and reach Indie Annie's inbox at IndieAnnie@indieauthormagazine.com. Finally, interact with us and other authors at https://indieauthortraining.com/groups. We love hearing new voices and can't wait to continue learning alongside you.

Nicole Schroeder
Editor in Chief
Indie Author Magazine

Nicole Schroeder is a storyteller at heart. As the editor in chief of Indie Author Magazine, she brings nearly a decade of journalism and editorial experience to the publication, delighting in any opportunity to tell true stories and help others do the same. She holds a bachelor's degree from the Missouri School of Journalism and minors in English and Spanish. Her previous work includes editorial roles at local publications, and she's helped edit and produce numerous fiction and nonfiction books, including a Holocaust survivor's memoir, alongside independent publishers. Her own creative writing has been published in national literary magazines. When she's not at her writing desk, Nicole is usually in the saddle, cuddling her guinea pigs, or spending time with family. She loves any excuse to talk about Marvel movies and considers National Novel Writing Month its own holiday.

929 PRESS

Empowering Storytellers in a Digital Landscape

WE HELP STORYTELLERS BLEND THEIR ART WITH INNOVATIVE DIGITAL TOOLS TO CAPTIVATE AUDIENCES ACROSS ALL PLATFORMS

- EBook, Print & Audiobook Design & Formatting

- iOS and Google Play Apps

- Digital & Print Magazine Design & Distribution

- Website Design & Social Media Branding

929PRESS.COM

When Authors Should Go Global

As the book market becomes ever more global, the idea of offering translations of their work intrigues many authors. Ethan Ellenberg, a New York-based literary agent who works with a number of the Alliance of Independent Authors's (ALLi's) top authors—those who are part of ALLi's Authorpreneur membership and sell twenty-five-thousand-plus books a year or a business equivalent—says that foreign rights can bring in 20 percent to 30 percent of a top author's income, so translations are well worth planning for as your business grows.

But the considerations differ depending on where you are in your author business. In this article, we explore considerations for beginner authors, emerging authors, and experienced authors.

BEGINNER AUTHORS: GET INFORMED ABOUT THE INTERNATIONAL MARKET

For beginner authors, translations should probably not be high on your to-do list. You have enough to do with publishing multiple formats—e-book, print, and audio—in your own language, and all that entails. Even if you have time to explore other options, you may not have the budget, often in the range of $5,000, to commission your own book translations, and not enough book sales (yet!) to interest a foreign publisher.

So should you ignore opportunities in translations? No; use this time to gain an understanding of the translation market and how it is developing.

Investigate which indie authors, especially those in your genre, are pursuing translations, in which languages, and how it is working for them. Stay informed so that you can strike when the time is right.

You can tap into ALLi's complete guide to translations, which includes case studies from authors who have already built translation into their business, on the ALLi blog: https://selfpublishingadvice.org/the-ultimate-guide-to-book-translations-for-indie-authors.

EMERGING AUTHORS: ASSESS YOUR GOALS AND YOUR BUDGET

Once you've established yourself as a professional author, with your content available in multiple formats in your own language, you might consider whether translations are something you want to pursue and how.

What makes the most sense for your books? Interest in certain languages is sometimes driven by genre; for example, some indie authors have found great success with Historical Romance in German. Also factor in considerations like a book's setting; a book set in France might lend itself well to a French translation. Finally, keep in mind which languages have the greatest global application, such as Spanish.

Once you have identified target languages, you need to decide whether you want to produce the translation yourself, work with a professional translator, or license translation rights if you have already proven the book does well in English markets. When making this decision, factor in that translating the book itself is not the only work needed. For example, you may need to run ads in that language.

Make a careful assessment of the likely return on investment of pursuing translations, and don't let "shiny object syndrome" lure you into diving into the translation market without doing your homework first.

EXPERIENCED AUTHORS: BUILD TRANSLATIONS INTO YOUR BUSINESS PLAN

For those authors whose businesses are more developed and are enjoying robust book sales, translations are a great way to expand your earnings without having to write another word. For such busy authors, translation rights licensing can be an attractive option. This can enable you to offload much of the work not only of producing the translation but also of all the extra administrative, marketing, and promotion work that translation entails.

It's far from easy to promote work in a foreign language and unfamiliar territory. Getting local reviews, having a social media presence, optimizing your website for multiple languages, and ensuring you are meeting different cultural expectations and avoiding any taboos are all challenging.

The more experienced you are, the more books you are likely to have as candidates for translations. This opens the possibility of greater payback, but it also increases the complexity not only of managing your portfolio of translations but also of keeping your global audience engaged with you long-term.

Book covers, for example, vary considerably in style by country, which is why you often see books with different covers for US and UK markets. Reference this ALLi guide on global book distribution for more information: https://selfpublishingadvice.org/global-book-distribution-for-indie-authors.

Find out more about rights licensing in ALLi's guidebook *How Authors Sell Publishing Rights*, available through ALLi's online bookshop at https://selfpublishingadvice.org/bookshop.

AI TRANSLATION

Authors at all levels need to track changes to the translation landscape carefully, especially with the advent of AI. There has been lots of conversation about how AI might be used by authors and publishers to create translations of their books, but there is also the possibility that AI tools may eliminate the need for authors and publishers to do this work themselves. It's not difficult to imagine a world where any reader can read a work written in any language in their own language through a generic translation tool. It's also easy to imagine that, as with audiobooks, AI might provide dramatically more content across languages but that more nuanced human translations will still be desired and might command a premium price.

Track all the opportunities offered by translations with ALLi's comprehensive guide "The Ultimate Guide to Book Translations for Indie Authors" on the organization's blog. ◼

Matty Dalrymple, ALLi Campaigns Manager

Matty Dalrymple, ALLi Campaigns Manager

The Alliance of Independent Authors (ALLi) is a global membership association for self-publishing authors. A non-profit, our mission is ethics and excellence in self-publishing. Everyone on our team is a working indie author and we offer advice and advocacy for self-publishing authors within the literary, publishing and creative industries around the world.
www.allianceindependentauthors.org

Alliance of Independent Authors

Dear Indie Annie,

I've just hired a new cover designer for my series, but English is not their first language. I want to make the process run smoothly. Any tips for working around a language barrier?

Lost in Translation

Dear Lost in Translation,

Oh, poppet, collaborating across cultures can feel as daunting as decoding hieroglyphics! But with patience and open communication, you can transcend language barriers. View this as a thrilling expedition with your design sherpa!

What you need, my dear, is your very own Rosetta Stone. It may take a few attempts to decode your communicative challenges, but if you love this designer's work and they are practically perfect in every way for your little books, then it's worth the effort. Bridging creative divides across cultures takes finesse, but clear communication paves the way. Let's map out strategies for a fruitful, cross-pollinating collaboration!

First and foremost, lead with empathy and patience. Your designer is already operating outside their language comfort zone, so make them feel at ease. Default to kindness over bluntness when providing feedback. Deliver notes delicately, framing opinions as preferences: "I'm drawn to this style, but I'm curious about your take?" Encourage continued efforts despite any frustrations you may have. Remain positive—for example, say "Another approach could be …" rather than invoking negatives like "This isn't working!"

Establish common ground by sharing samples that represent your desired aesthetic. Images truly are the universal language. Provide lots of visual inspiration—covers you love, branding guidelines, and even mood boards to convey your aesthetic vision without ambiguity.

Dare I suggest you use AI tools to express the ideas you have? A picture paints a thousand words, as they say. Put your emphasis on showing rather than telling—not poor advice for your books either, my dear—and use pictorial examples to reinforce adjectives like "vibrant," "modern," etc.

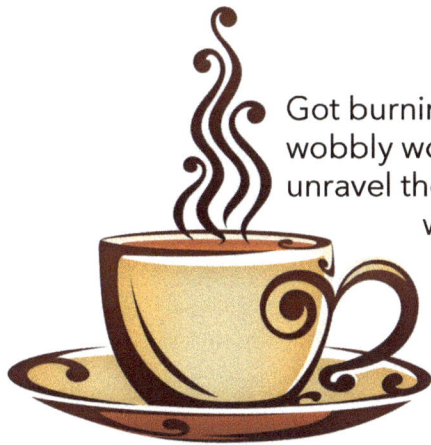

Got burning questions about the wibbly-wobbly world of indie authoring? Eager to unravel the mysteries of publishing, writing woes, or anything in between? Give your quizzical quills a whirl and shoot your musings over to indieannie@ indieauthormagazine.com. Your inky quandaries are my cup of tea!

Eliminate as much translation guesswork as possible upfront. Before starting, take time to define design terminology on both sides clearly. Walk through concepts like "layout," "motif," and "tone," and ensure you share a mutual understanding of these meanings. If there appears to be confusion, consider affordable, or even free, online translation services, and hire a professional interpreter for critical feedback exchanges.

Maintain an open spirit to fresh creative perspectives. Your designer's outside vantage point may inspire innovative new directions you would never have considered. Celebrate this cultural exchange throughout the process, not just the final product.

Establish a transparent feedback loop and communication cadence. Determine if ongoing video chats with visuals or documented comments work best. Consider collaboration tools like Google Docs to integrate input seamlessly. Agree on reasonable turnaround times.

And, unlike your sweet aunt Indie, try to steer clear of overly complex sentences and flowery language. I am writing for effect. I am your sweet-natured literary godmother, employed to be grandiose in my vocabulary.

You, on the other hand, sweet lost child, are embarking on a journey that requires the strategic use of the simplest words in your lexicon—unless, of course, you find that even with English as their second language, it's still better than yours!

Most of all, extend grace and good faith from start to finish. This partnership will strengthen empathy and expand both of your visions. Ahead of you lies an exciting exploratory adventure as enriching as the book journeys you script. With mutual patience and goodwill, you can traverse any linguistic landscape. Now, get out those proverbial pens and maps; new creative vistas await, no translation required!

Happy writing,
Indie Annie X

10 TIPS FOR
LOCAL EVENTS

One of the first rules of marketing any indie author learns is to identify your ideal reader. You build an avatar of the person you're writing for: their age, gender, socioeconomic status, interests, habits, and anything else you can think of that will help you visualize and personalize your audience. Then you use that avatar to target readers with bonus content, social media, and ads.

Sometimes, meeting your reader where they are means reaching out in person. Authors often consider book fairs, readings, and library events first, but many readers' interests go beyond bookish events. If your ideal reader is the kind of person who attends Comic Con, farmers' markets, or craft fairs, it makes sense for you to be there, too. Middle-grade fiction author Melisa Torres, who writes about young gymnasts, attends youth gymnastic events, offering signed books to the All-Around winner of each session.

Attending these niche events gives authors an opportunity to broaden their reader base but may require a shift in mindset. Instead of being one of many authors pitching an audience who are already interested in purchasing books, you may be the only one selling them, for better or worse. "One thing you do have to be prepared for is not everyone reads, and not everyone will read your genre. So don't be offended when people aren't into books. I once had someone tell me they would rather go to the dentist than read a book at a big regional vendor event," says Liz Delton, Fantasy author.

In speaking with several authors who have found success in less reader-focused venues, a few tips stood out. Here are some things you should know before you register for the next street festival.

WHAT TO BRING

(1) TABLE SETUP

Depending on the venue, you may need to bring your own table, chairs, and/or tent. Decorate your space to draw attention, and use levels to display your books with visual interest. Provide clear and accurate signage with your prices, socials, and a way to sign up for your newsletter; consider creating a poster or business cards with a QR code to make it easier. Make it clear you are the author, as guests may be excited to meet you. Lean into that published author mystique.

(2) BOOKS

Since you're probably engaging with a cold audience, emphasize books that offer easy entry into your collection, usually first in series. Bring fewer copies of the rest, but have them available for readers who like to purchase complete sets. You may also want to have some books pre-signed and packaged for guests who are in a hurry. Have a stack of Post-Its and a pen nearby for people to write down the name they'd like you to use for inscriptions. Experienced authors suggest you bring more than you think you'll need so you don't sell out, but the exact number will depend on you (your display and sales techniques), your books (covers and blurbs), and the event (how well it matches your reader profile).

Pro Tip: "Track your own analytics. Keep track of the size of the event, demographics, and which books sold. Figure out the percentage of books sold in relation to the size of the event. Then you can fine-tune which books, and how many, to bring next time," Torres says.

(3) GOODIES

Giveaways like candy, bookmarks, pens, and business cards will help people remember you and encourage them to stop. Guests who don't buy your book may take something to pass on to reader friends. "Kids love stickers and bookmarks. Even if your books aren't for kids, if the kids stop, the parents stop," says Lori Briley Fairchild, author of YA and children's books. Selling secondary products like stickers, pins, and character art increases your potential income and provides opportunities for bundling with your books, which adds value to in-person sales.

(4) WATER

Remember to hydrate, even if the venue is indoors. Sales events can be physically taxing, and you want to keep your energy up to welcome anyone who stops by your table.

(5) MONEY

You're here to sell books, so make sure you have a reliable way to accept cash. You'll need a bank to make change and somewhere to store it securely. Or go cash free with a Square device, PayPal, or Venmo. Just make sure to bring chargers and a source of backup power in case you aren't near an outlet.

WHAT TO DO

(6) PLAN AHEAD

Some events need to be registered well in advance, so start tracking deadlines early. Consider trying different events as opposed to repeatedly visiting weekly or monthly markets to avoid seeing some of the same people week to week. Choose events that relate to your niche, where the other vendors sell products that align with your brand. If the entry fee is a challenge, consider sharing a booth. Be on time, and prepare to stay until the end. Acknowledge that events can be physically and mentally draining, and plan for rest time and recovery afterward.

Pro Tip: Don't leave for lunch. Mystery and Sci-Fi author Judith A. Barrett says she gets the highest traffic at farmers' markets and arts and crafts shows between 11 a.m. and 1 p.m.

(7) MAKE A STRONG FIRST IMPRESSION

When at your booth, stand up if you're able to, or bring a tall stool to make yourself more visible and approachable. Put your phone away unless you're actively using it for a sale.

Embrace your brand, and be consistent with it. Dress for the occasion in comfortable clothes and good shoes, but remember where you are and consider how you might use your appearance to grab attention or start conversations: costumes at a renaissance faire, graphic tees with geeky references at a con.

Smile. "Don't get mad every time someone passes by your table or doesn't buy anything—it will add up to a miserable experience for you and everyone who interacts with you. First impressions are everything!" says Audrey Hughey, founder of the Author Transformation Alliance and *IAM* staff writer.

(8) HONE YOUR PITCH

With any in-person event, you only have a few seconds to grab a reader's attention, but if you're attending an event that isn't built around books, you'll need to know your angle. How do your books relate to the vibe of the event? What do your characters have in common with the other vendors and guests? Gauge interest, make a connection, and give people space to participate in the conversation instead of launching into an extended spiel.

9 EMPLOY PSYCHOLOGY

Check your breathing. Long exhales stimulate your vagus nerve, signaling your nervous system to relax. Once you have your own energy under control, observe the event attendees. What do you notice about the demographics, relationships, and interests of the people making purchases? Ask open-ended questions to encourage them to stop and talk. Engage them in conversations about the details you've noticed—"Nice Iron Man shirt! Which Marvel movie is your favorite?"—and listen to what they say. Look for commonalities to personalize their experience, such as, "Your granddaughter likes to read? I write YA books! How old is she?" Mirroring some of their body language may subconsciously build rapport.

---

10 STAY POSITIVE

Acknowledge and include everyone who shows interest in your table, even if it's just a simple shift in your stance when someone new comes up. Non-author-focused events may be hit or miss for immediate sales since you're not facing an audience entirely composed of readers, but you never know when people will take your card and give it to a friend or purchase something as a gift. Befriend the other vendors when you aren't talking to your guests. On top of promoting a positive attitude and fostering a welcoming space, you may make a connection that leads to more events and more sales. After all, vendors are readers, too.

Pro Tip: For more guidance, Epic Fantasy author Angel Haze recommends Ben Wolf's *Power Author: Mastering Live Events.* ■

Jenn Lessmann

Jenn Lessmann

Jenn Lessmann is the author of Unmagical: a Witchy Mystery and three stories on Kindle Vella. A former barista, stage manager, and high school English teacher with advanced degrees from impressive colleges, she continues to drink excessive amounts of caffeine, stay up later than is absolutely necessary, and read three or four books at a time. Jenn is currently studying witchcraft and the craft of writing, and giggling internally whenever they intersect. She writes snarky paranormal fantasy for new adults whenever her dog will allow it.

Seven-Figure Stanzas

HOW DIRECT SALES AND TRANSMEDIA HAVE HELPED PIERRE ALEX JEANTY'S POETRY SOAR

Thought-provoking poetry can speak to readers around the world. It's something people have seemingly always innately understood about the art form, and it's a fact Pierre Alex Jeanty has witnessed firsthand as he's helped his readers gain inspiration and strength to love and grow. But the impact of Pierre's poetry has gone beyond his readers. Over the past ten years, he has transformed the idea behind those books—to love yourself and what you do—into a full-fledged business model for authors to emulate in order to take their business to new heights.

A bestselling, multi-seven-figure author of poetry who specializes in selling his books directly to readers, Pierre is also the owner of 7 Figure Book Business, helping authors through courses and accelerators to leave behind the idea of "authorpreneurship" and instead drive their focus toward building a sustainable business. Pierre also operates a Facebook Ads agency for authors and a warehousing and distribution service for authors embracing direct sales.

Pierre started his career as an influencer, having built an audience on social media at the time to the tune of fifty thousand followers on Instagram, five hundred thousand followers on X—then called Twitter—and one hundred thousand on Facebook. His brand was called "Gentlemenhood" and offered online advice to men. Then his following started asking him to write a book. He wrote his first book in 2014 and started with one hundred preorders.

By the end of the month, he had sold five hundred copies.

From there, he started writing poetry online using social media, which allowed him to appeal to a wider audience and build his poetry brand from scratch. Now, his business has grown to over two hundred thousand customers on his list and millions of followers across his various social media channels. He has an author website built for e-commerce and has become his own Amazon storefront. He drives all traffic to his website from social media and ads, and now, he has the customer data he needs to make wise business decisions.

A MARKET-AWARE MINDSET

Pierre largely attributes his success to knowing how to build an audience before he published his first book. As he started advertising, he made sure to write in a way that worked with Facebook's 20 percent text rule. This rule, expunged in 2021, said that for an ad to be approved on the platform, the ad image couldn't consist of more than 20 percent text. Pierre's ads for his poetry books fit perfectly within the rule's guidelines, and he was able to write books that were easy to market within Facebook's ecosystem because of this deliberate formatting.

When asked about the lessons he learned in the process of building his business, he says at first, he didn't realize he was an indie author. "I was a marketer who knew how to grow on social media," he says. "I knew how to listen to my audience, and I want others to adopt the business mindset I had at the beginning." Pierre's mindset is counterintuitive to a lot of common teachings in the indie author ecosystem. He focuses on building an audi-

ence outside of Amazon, focusing on the customer journey and implementing traditional business practices that don't fuel the algorithm but rather fuel his business.

"Everything is becoming more competitive. Things aren't lasting outside of individual communities where there is no control," he says. "Platforms are changing faster, and if you don't have control, you'll fall behind."

Pierre's thoughts on connecting with readers go beyond email marketing. Instead, he utilizes social media and user-generated content (UGC) to sell his books. "People sell to people, not just through ads, and if you want control of that, then show your face. TikTok set a standard for non-advertising appearance. People want to meet real people. That's why livestreams work so well—because you're speaking directly to readers."

Speaking directly to readers, stepping out from behind the computer, and becoming the face of your business might sound terrifying for some, but for Pierre, it's led to a business model that is more hands-on than most and a daily routine he enjoys. He spends a lot of time focused on building his business and less on writing, but that also means his writing is more focused and purposeful. He has a small team that helps him manage, package, and ship books for himself and other authors he works with.

A BRAND BUILT ON READERS

In a digital-first world, plenty of indie authors focus their energy on e-books and audiobooks before turning to print. Pierre's focus is on print books and

product boxes containing T-shirts and other branded merchandise. He has an office like most, but his business is largely hands-off—besides managing his Facebook ads. Customers purchase a book directly from his website, built on Shopify, and his warehouse receives the order and fulfills it. Customer service has also been turned over to his team, and he prefers to delegate tasks to his employees with the help of standard operating procedures and workflows, such as how to pack and order.

He says his focus on products such as workbooks and T-shirts are complementary to his books and allow him to act as a brand builder.

"Harry Potter is a good example [of this]," he says. "Big brands used to be the only ones capable of merchandising, but now, you can build a community who support the products because they have a connection to the story that sells the product."

Authors and other business owners can source merchandise in small enough batches that it is economic, and the financial risk is a lot less, Pierre says. But this direct-first model may not be for everybody. Pierre's focus is on building a brand presence tied to his products and being a direct line between his brand and his customers.

Pierre suggests direct sales are for authors who are looking at the long-term results of building a business, which counters the traditional Amazon model focused on digital sales. "Print is a massive market, and customers experience excitement when they get their books in the mail," he says. But it can also differ by genre. "If a book appeals to a larger market and the author adopts a business mindset first, they can sell their story. Selling direct can work in the extremes, niche or super broad, because the customers are easier to target."

Pierre says authors, especially new authors, should think of their books as products first. Authors shouldn't write without a goal and instead should remember the consumer and go into it looking to sell products and merchandise. A book without the audience in mind is a passion project, he says, but a book written for an audience is a product.

To find out what an audience wants, Pierre has a solution.

"Survey your audience," he says. "Write about their struggles and what it feels like to be them. Pull from your experience and answer questions for the audience in your books."

A CHANGING LANDSCAPE

Over time, Pierre's business has transformed to the point his struggles are also different. He said in the beginning, he focused on growth and scale while maintaining communication with his audience. Now, his troubles are less author related as more business responsibilities arise and he sets his eyes on a new goal: $4 million in sales for the year. Pierre said his personal goals have also changed. He doesn't write everyday anymore, and instead he focuses on the joys of owning a business, working with his team, and teaching and helping other authors grow.

The landscape of publishing is changing, and Pierre is but one of many authors who have considered how direct sales can fit into their publishing model. "Owning your community and selling your own products is the new creator economy," Pierre says. His focus on building a community, writing for the reader, and owning your audience is sound advice for new and seasoned authors alike. ∎

David Viergutz

David Viergutz

David Viergutz is a disabled Army Veteran, Law Enforcement Veteran, husband and proud father. He is an author of stories from every flavor of horror and dark fiction. One day, David's wife sat him down and gave him the confidence to start putting his imagination on paper. From then on out his creativity has no longer been stifled by self-doubt and he continues to write with a smile on his face in a dark, candle-lit room.

From Creatives to Content Creators

REFLECTIONS FROM THE CONTENT ENTREPRENEUR EXPO 2024

Attending a conference is always a game-changing experience, offering new ideas, invaluable networking, and insights into trends and new technology. From May 5–7, more than 350 people gathered at the Hotel Cleveland in Cleveland, Ohio, for exactly that at the Content Entrepreneur Expo (CEX). Sponsored by Lulu and many other industry names, this conference was intended for a broad audience of creators: bloggers, podcasters, authors, newsletter writers, speakers, coaches, consultants, freelancers, and YouTubers. And it offered something for everyone.

I write novels. Unlike many other people attending CEX, I don't have a side hustle in social media. I don't market for other people, I don't blog, and I'm still finding my feet as an author entrepreneur. Yet there I was, ready to meet and greet and put myself out there at CEX, where the itinerary focused on building revenue and audiences without relying on Big Tech, learning how to use AI, and connecting with other content entrepreneurs.

Comfort zones, shmumfort zones.

How did a neurodivergent and introverted author get here, you might ask? I had never heard of CEX until I was offered a ticket through my position as a volunteer with Author Nation. The opportunity meant I got to see a professional conference from the attendee side, but it also meant I got to meet other people doing adjacent work and expand my proverbial horizons.

From the big ideas to the hands-on sessions, there was so much to learn. The central idea I took away for fellow authors, however? Authors are content creators, and we should explore what works and what doesn't as we pivot with the changing market and audience preferences. It's not just books on a giant storefront fighting for eyeballs—or it doesn't have to be.

HIGHLIGHTS

One key takeaway from many of the sessions was a phrase we have all likely heard: "Don't build on rented land." In this case, it means that anything you build in a space you don't own isn't actually yours. If your favorite platform stopped working tomorrow, would you have access to your fans? Would your access to your reader community be lost? There were multiple sessions on email marketing, memberships, and newsletters intended to help people take back their own content and audiences.

Another idea that was repeated throughout the event was the importance of diversified revenue streams. Authors are succeeding in different formats, such as on YouTube, with merchandise and experiences in their own stores, as affiliates, on crowdfunding platforms, and with paid newsletters and memberships in communities. This expands on the idea of owning your audience communication and your tech stack.

There was also a whole track on Tuesday dedicated to AI. Although we learned to "ChatGPT it!" when we got stuck setting up our digital doppelgänger—then called that out whenever a speaker paused for an answer through the rest of the conference—there were many other sessions that introduced AI tools, taught us how to better use programs we were already familiar with, or helped make current content more searchable and relevant. Most of this was new to me, but seeing how AI can do the grunt work while leaving creators free to create was compelling.

Other tracks focused on learning to drive revenue, audience growth, publishing, and social media. Each of these had a dedicated room on one day, with sessions targeted toward that topic. As an indie author and business owner, I found myself at different levels of competence on these tracks, and like many attendees, I ended up skipping around the tracks depending on which sessions drew my interest. After sessions spent learning more about community building, I felt much better equipped to build the foundation for community in my business, whether it is a subscription model or crowdfunding.

Our first session was a workshop given by Andrew Davis called, "Maximize your Speaking Success as a Referable Speaker: A Masterclass." It really was a masterclass. I have no plans to become a full-time speaker, but listening to the methodology and tips gave me so much insight into the process. It also highlighted the importance of connecting with others, as Davis demonstrated, using real numbers, how stage-side leads after his speeches drive and increase his business. We always hear about the importance of networking, but this was a concrete demonstration of the outcome. We were later treated to another session with this speaker, and I'd highly recommend any speech by him—a fitting endorsement of the lessons he taught in his first session.

As with many conferences, meeting new people is key to getting the most out of the experience. There were big names and newbies, and everyone was open to talking and collaborating. Longer breaks between sessions and seating groups in the common space allowed attendees to speak with other creators. The social events, including an '80s themed party, were great fun. And attending with a team of fantastic people, all of whom are knowledgeable and dedicated to the conference we will put on later this year, added a twist to our already delicious conference martini.

There were so many fantastic speakers, it feels necessary to list a few other highlights: Creator Science founder Jay Clouse gave a great session on prioritizing longform content, which is particularly relevant to novel writers and other longer-form authors who are creating intellectual property and owning their distribution channels as an enduring asset. Author Nation Managing Director Joe Solari gave a thought-provoking talk on identifying and building your audience in a challenging market. Author Bonnie Paulson shared a worksheet and hands-on session on building your online community. And the keynote speaker was B.J. Novak, an author, actor, and comedian, who was interviewed by Ann Handley and discussed audience expectations, creative integrity, and an unconventional career. There were so many good sessions that I can't mention them all.

OTHER NOTES

The publishing track offered tips for authors who are at the very beginning of their publishing experience, ideal for those who are stepping into it fresh. As someone who has published several books already, I found the other tracks offered more new-to-me information. The sponsor booths, including Lulu, Ecamm, Teach:able, Thinkific, Memberful, and ConvertKit, were relevant and convenient. Overall, it was a mix of anecdotal and inspirational talks with practical, step-by-step sessions. The scope started with big ideas and worked down to details. There were options for everyone, no matter the type of content you create or your level.

For authors like myself, CEX felt particularly relevant to those expanding from simply selling books. There were sessions and people who could speak to each level of the process, whether you were merely observing the options or had already moved on them. Author conferences absolutely have their place in any author's repertoire, but going outside the author conference box can spark ideas and get your creativity flowing. It certainly did for all the attendees I spoke with.

For 2024, CEX cost $395 for online access approximately two weeks after the event; $795 for access to the sessions, lunches and snacks, and evening parties; and $1,095 for an all-access pass, which included a preconference workshop and VIP networking party, in addition to the in-person sessions and recordings. CEX has been held yearly for the last three years, and though location and dates have not been announced yet for 2025, digital passes to the 2024 content were still available at press time. Watch the event's website, https://cex.events, for updates about next year's event and information on how to register. ■

Jen B. Green

Jen B. Green

Jen B. Green has lived in five countries on four continents with her three sons, two daughters, and one great guy. She reads anything that stays still long enough, plays piano, and bakes everything sweet.

After earning her Ph.D. in psychology, Jen tried writing a novel for Nanowrimo and was hooked! Her days are spent traveling the world, teaching undergraduate psychology, and wrangling her growing homemade army, but her nights are for writing Urban Fantasy with witches and werewolves.

PUBLISHERROCKET

FIND
PROFITABLE
KINDLE
KEYWORDS

Book Marketing Research
Made Simple!

writelink.to/pubrocket

First Subscriptions for Authors Summit a Unicorn among Author Events

Most days, the Artists For Humanity EpiCenter in South Boston, Massachusetts, hosts local teenage artists and their professional mentors. In the non-profit's open venue, amid canvas paintings hung along the walls and artwork made of reclaimed windshields that line the walkway on the second floor, students from underprivileged communities work alongside others in the industry to create commissioned projects, fostering their creativity in the process.

On May 6 and 7, the space fostered the creativity of approximately seventy authors as well, as the home of the first Subscriptions for Authors (SFA) Summit hosted by Ream co-founders Michael Evans and Emilia Rose and SFA Summit manager Anna McCluskey.

Evans's mantra for managing a successful author subscription, to "under-promise and over-deliver," was quoted at several points in the conference, but it also became the perfect way to encapsulate the event. The two-day experience featured ten sessions by innovators in the indie author community and two panel discussions from a diverse set of authors, as well as smaller breakout sessions, a bonus keynote, and an after-hours chat with Evans himself that was equal parts advice, stories of Ream's start, and unicorn jokes. Although the summit promised discussions related to all things subscriptions, the lessons shared spoke to all manner of authors at every stage of their business, from those not yet published to those with more than sixty books to their name. Beyond a space that fostered the creativity of

Ream co-founder Michael Evans speaks to attendees on day 1 of the Subscriptions for Authors Summit, held May 6 and 7 in Boston, Massachusetts.

Tonya Kappes shares stories from her author career as part of a session on maintaining a successful subscription.

attendees—who were able to spend time between sessions conversing about and admiring the artwork on the walls—the summit fostered community and connection, too, whether it be with readers, with industry professionals, or with other attendees.

DAY 1: FOR THE FANS

With only two days' worth of content, speakers spent little time introducing the subscription model to attendees; day 1 of the summit dived straight into exploring a variety of subscription strategies. Ream co-founder Emilia Rose highlighted her subscription model centered on her characters and story worlds, and Tonya Kappes shared the content she offers her readers that's as much about her as it is her stories. "I am my brand," she said to start off her talk.

Perhaps the most universal lesson shared by speakers was to match your business model to your current "season" in life, as Katlyn Duncan said during the "Subscriptions for Y'all" panel. Stephanie Berchiolly, as part of the same panel, called out "toxic productivity culture" as a reason many authors feel the need to burn themselves out rather than adapting their business to what is most sustainable for them.

Later in the afternoon, focus returned to readers with discussions about the concept of fandoms and how to find superfans among your readers. As the day wrapped up, Sci-Fi author and creator of the "Hopperverse" Christopher Hopper turned his session into a demonstration of the idea. As he shared how trading cards, poker chips, and challenge coins united his fandom, he made his own reveal to the audience, Oprah-style, that special edition cards had been taped underneath their seats for them to take home—turning Ream's own Evans into a hero in his stories' universe.

"The entire place fell out with laughter," says Sci-Fi and Fantasy author Kacey Ezell, who called the moment her favorite part of the summit. "[There was] a lot of really good energy. It was super fun."

The night continued with dinner breakout sessions that became bonding experiences for attendees and a chance to share one-on-one advice, as well as after-hours sessions that were truly more informal chats between speakers and the audience than presentations. In his talk, Evans—sporting a Ream "Romance Authors Rule the World" basketball jersey—shared lessons he'd learned from Ream's beginning that authors could apply in their own careers, as well as a fair number of stories from his own life outside of writing. Although some took notes, most of the audience who'd lasted that far into the evening simply listened and laughed.

Those in attendance connected with Katlyn Duncan's message of modifying your writing schedule based on your "season" in life.

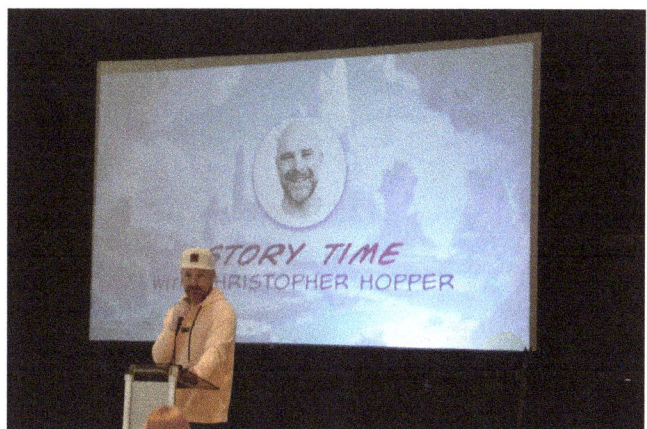

Christopher Hopper's session on acknowledging your superfans was a favorite among many of the summit attendees, bringing Hopper's enthusiasm and a surprise reveal to the group to round out the first day of sessions before evening salons and after-hours events.

DAY 2: FOR THE AUTHORS

The conference's second day focused even more on authors' relationships with their readers, as well as preserving your own mental health. Author Sarra Cannon, who also hosts the Heart Breathings YouTube channel, emphasized putting readers first when creating content and building trust with your audience, and Horror author and *IAM* contributor David Viergutz explored author branding as a promise to the reader. At the close of the day, author Nora Phoenix offered attendees advice on giving themselves grace with examples from her own writing journey, provoking a few tears from audience members as she suggested a shift from asking "What if I fail?" to "What if I succeed?"

The lessons resonated with Urban Fantasy and Sci-Fi author Lara Magill. "I have to set boundaries for myself if I ever hope to live up to the goals and the standards that I want to achieve," she says. "But also, a big part of that is not just respecting me and my boundaries but also understanding my readers, what they need, what they want, and how I can deliver those expectations in a sustainable way."

The sessions and panels as the event continued reflected the closeness attendees had gained even from the day before. Audience members shared their shock when Viergutz admitted to having killed off a dog in the first pages of one of his books, and other speakers referenced stories from audience members they'd met at breakout sessions the day before. The connections people made weren't restrained by genre, skill level, or marketing strategy; in fact, by the time people broke for genre-specific luncheons, Sci-Fi, Horror, and Fantasy authors—roughly a third of the conference—opted to walk to the same restaurant during the break and swapped advice and business cards along the way.

As Evans closed out the event late Tuesday afternoon, he elaborated on the future of Subscriptions for Authors and the in-person summit. Having announced Bookshops on Ream the weekend before the event, he expanded on the changes coming to Ream, as well as the rebrand from Subscriptions for Authors to Storytellers Rule the World (STRW), to audience members.

With several new features planned to launch over the next year, Evans said there were no current plans to host another in-person event—an announcement that many were disappointed with after the success of the summit. However, the STRW community remains active in the Subscriptions for Authors Facebook Group, and the *Storytellers Rule the World Show* releases new podcast episodes each week. For those interested in exploring subscription models, both are spaces to watch for announcements about new features and—hopefully—future events in 2025 and beyond. ◼

Nicole Schroeder

Some of the artwork on display at the Artists for Humanity EpiCenter.

Sarra Cannon elaborates on the importance of developing trust with your readers on day 2 of the SFA Summit.

Not every session focused solely on subscription platforms. David Viergutz spoke in his session about creating a consistent and clear author brand.

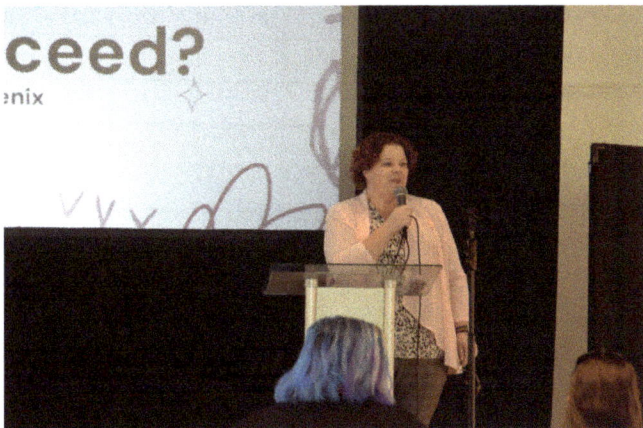

The final session on the summit's second day brought some attendees to tears as Nora Phoenix asked, "What is the voice in your head telling you?"

Evans talks about the future of the Subscriptions for Authors Summit and what's in store for Storytellers Rule the World in 2024 and beyond.

Nicole Schroeder

Nicole Schroeder is a storyteller at heart. As the editor in chief of Indie Author Magazine, she brings nearly a decade of journalism and editorial experience to the publication, delighting in any opportunity to tell true stories and help others do the same. She holds a bachelor's degree from the Missouri School of Journalism and minors in English and Spanish. Her previous work includes editorial roles at local publications, and she's helped edit and produce numerous fiction and nonfiction books, including a Holocaust survivor's memoir, alongside independent publishers. Her own creative writing has been published in national literary magazines. When she's not at her writing desk, Nicole is usually in the saddle, cuddling her guinea pigs, or spending time with family. She loves any excuse to talk about Marvel movies and considers National Novel Writing Month its own holiday.

An Author's New Translation Tool?

WHETHER AI CAN HELP YOU PRODUCE TRANSLATIONS CHEAPER

From direct sales to AI-generated audiobooks, technology is rapidly advancing, opening doors to new publishing mediums that were all but closed to most authors in recent years. Those seeking opportunities to reach new audiences often turn to translations, making further use of their intellectual property by getting their books translated into foreign languages and targeting other markets that may be underserved. However, this has its own issues—most notably that hiring professional human translators can be cost-prohibitive. Some authors are at an impasse, either unable to afford a quality translation and ignoring the market entirely or turning to less-experienced editors to find their investment squelched by poor reviews. But there is a middle ground rising from the world of artificial intelligence. Large language models such as DeepL and ChatGPT are making strides in translating English into foreign languages.

Authors are using this technology by combining it with human proofreaders or editors of the translated language who can catch the errors you can't, ensuring accuracy while cutting down on costs. This middle ground in the AI versus human translation debate gives both arguments credence by employing humans, one of the primary arguments against AI, and utilizing the efficiency of technology, one of the primary arguments in support of it.

But while this use case might seem like a happy medium, there are still questions left unanswered.

Who owns the rights to the work when both AI and human editors are involved? How trustworthy is the method really, and does it trade financial cost for more time away from other projects? Whatever your publishing path is, when exploring translating your books into foreign languages, you should always understand your options, opportunities, and considerations as it pertains to your intellectual property. Explored are a few options for making your book available in other languages.

HUMAN TRANSLATORS

Often viewed as the most expensive option, authors often seek qualified translators from word-of-mouth referrals, job-posting boards such as Fiverr and Reedsy, or through translation service agencies. Once a translator has been selected and the terms agreed upon, authors work collaboratively with the translator to transform their book from one language into another. This process takes the largest amount of time and thus is the most expensive. The price to employ a translator is often a concern for budget-conscious authors, ranging on average between $0.08 to $0.12 a word, or $6,700 to $9,600 for an eighty-thousand-word manuscript, according to Reedsy.

The time necessary to translate a book ranges, but authors should be prepared for the project to reach fruition in weeks if not months. As with any collaboration, a translator may request the author participate in the process via video conferences, emails, or messages to discuss issues or preferences as they arise. Once the manuscript has been produced, authors might seek a beta reader for the translated manuscript, as with any kind of edit, there is a likelihood for errors to slip through. This is an additional expense authors need to consider. Once the manuscript is at a finished stage, authors may incur additional expenses, such as alternative cover designs and book formatting, which should be factored into the author's overall budget for the project. As always, the author needs to consider the terms of the agreement with the translator and how it pertains to the intellectual property of the translated piece. Authors should be ready to read their contract end-to-end to ensure they know what they're signing.

FULL AI TRANSLATION

AI applications have seen an exponential uptick in development and capabilities in the last five years. Large language models (LLMs), generally the applications associated with AI technology, generate human-like text based on the prompts they receive, including translating existing writing into a new language. ChatGPT and DeepL are two applications capable of translating text, with an efficacy that seems to be improving.

Authors should refer to the specific application of their choice for more guidance but can generally expect to input a selection of text and ask the application via prompt to translate it into the language they desire. But while applications are improving, two problems arise when relying only on the application.

First, AI applications, specifically LLMs, can "hallucinate," or generate incorrect or made-up information while attempting to answer a question or complete a task. The application is attempting to generate plausible text based on patterns it has been trained upon, but it doesn't actually "know" the information asked of it. As a result, authors could receive parts of their manuscript where the application has hallucinated, or added in sections, words, or phrases that were never actually provided in the source text.

The second issue comes from the perspective of copyright—specifically, who owns the copyright to text generated by AI, even if the source material is the author's intellectual property. Even though legal discussions surrounding AI have been ongoing for more than a year, this area is still muddled, and further developments in the field of AI and copyrighted material are expected in the coming months.

Authors may see AI technology as the solution to the high expenditure of hiring human translators, but the other implications regarding property rights and consistency of the applications used still need to be considered. Also keep in mind that direct translations may not work in some genres or with certain idioms or phrases. Language contains nuances that AI technology may not be trained to see or translate. Those not fond of the idea of putting all their trust in an AI application or the expensive costs of a cover-to-cover translation may look to a hybrid of the two approaches.

PARTNERSHIP WITH AI AND A TRANSLATOR

Authors, whether working exclusively with a human translator or running their book through an AI application, can face pros and cons with both options for translating their work. However, there may be room for a hybrid of the two approaches.

In this case, an author would run their book or piece through an application, either in sections or in entirety, and pass off the manuscript to a translator for beta reading and quality control. Currently, AI can translate large amounts of text to varying degrees of success depending on the platform used, enough so that the time spent by the translator may be reduced. Authors can also expect lower costs than a full translation, though this can vary as the quality of output by the application also varies. Authors must still answer the questions surrounding intellectual property and their agreement with a translator, and are encouraged to review all documents before signing. For example, Joanna Penn found that in Germany, the copyright to the translated document belongs to the translator. However, if the first draft is created mostly by the author through AI, and that draft is then edited by a translator, the author maintains the copyright.

No matter the path an author chooses, exploring translations is a rich market of opportunity for making the most out of their intellectual property. Over time, AI technology is expected to improve, thus continuing to provide more options for authors to publish in other languages and countries that might have otherwise been inaccessible because of the costs of hiring translators. It's up to the authors themselves to explore all options and find what works best for their business. ■

David Viergutz

David Viergutz

David Viergutz is a disabled Army Veteran, Law Enforcement Veteran, husband and proud father. He is an author of stories from every flavor of horror and dark fiction. One day, David's wife sat him down and gave him the confidence to start putting his imagination on paper. From then on out his creativity has no longer been stifled by self-doubt and he continues to write with a smile on his face in a dark, candle-lit room.

Cover Your Bases

You are expanding your market base and audience by translating your books into foreign languages, and now you're ready to make a critical decision: do you keep your existing cover design, or do you create a new design that appeals to the new market?

We know how traditional publishers handle translations. They often create a different cover for each language, with some languages having small changes and others receiving a completely different cover. Translations already require a financial investment for both indie authors and traditional publishing companies, but an additional cover can add a new—and sometimes significant—cost to the decision.

Sticking with your current cover design may lead readers to recognize your book easier and align with your author brand whereas new covers could better appeal to your new target audience. There may be elements on your cover that need to be removed because they go against dominant cultural or religious beliefs in certain countries. There are other formatting issues to keep in mind as well, including languages that are read right to left, the hyphen-ation of foreign language words, and the need for accent marks or slight changes to the title text to make your cover text readable to your new audience, even if you stick with your original design.

What is the best choice for indie authors dipping their toes into translation and foreign markets? As always, there is no one-and-done way for indies to approach translations—but there are a few things you can consider before making the choice for your business.

E-BOOK COVERS

After finding a translator, many authors decide whether they want to convert their existing e-book's cover to the new language or invest funds in a new cover. Even though paperback books seem to be in higher demand in European countries, e-books still have a strong place in the market. If you're going to update your cover, the first place to start is with the e-book design since it will play a large part in the paperback.

But how do you know whether your existing cover will work in a new market?

Start by looking at popular e-books on Amazon in that specific country to see if your design and typography will work with other books in your genre. Then, consult with either your translator, since they should know the market as well, or an author who publishes in that language as their native language and would be willing to give advice on whether your cover would work for the language.

Changes may include what, if any, symbols are used on a cover, differences in colors, or even whether people are pictured. For some translated editions, especially those translated into Asian and Arabic languages, you might need to find a designer who can create a cover that meets the cultural and religious expectations of a particular country.

For other languages, your book's title, when translated, may not work with your current typography. You may have to consider either changing the layout of the typography or creating a cover that would work with the new title. Not all fonts have the diacritics, or accented characters, needed for foreign languages, so you may need to change your cover's fonts to be compatible. In addition, very few English fonts have characters to accommodate languages that don't use the Roman alphabet, like Japanese or Korean. If you want a prettier font in these languages, you may have to pay for a font with characters you like.

If it's not feasible to create new covers for each language, consider starting with languages where the only change that needs to be made is to the typography and then expand from there.

No matter what you decide, there will be other indie authors who are making the same decisions as you are. Self-Publishing Formula creator Mark Dawson has different covers for his books in English and German whereas 20BooksTo50K® co-founder Craig Martelle's English and German covers are the same except for the typography.

PAPERBACK COVERS

Unfortunately, it is rare that you can use the same paperback cover for your translated book as you did for the book in its original language. Often, there are additional pages in translated books, as well as additional back matter with the translator's information. It's also important to remember that, for some languages, like German, words on the spine are printed opposite from how English words are laid out. Any back cover text will likely need to be translated or reformatted as well.

Knowing how the spine and the back of the book should be laid out ahead of time can save you time and money on cover production. (As a translation cover designer, I always provide covers to the translator before finalizing them to make sure everything is formatted correctly.) Ask your cover designer if they will allow you to share a translated

WHY TRANSLATING YOUR BOOK MAY REQUIRE A COVER CHANGE—AND WHAT TO DO ABOUT IT

design with the translator to verify all is good before you finalize it.

INTERIOR FORMATTING

If you are used to formatting in English, you wouldn't know how rules change when formatting other languages. Unless you're told otherwise—and some software can't be told another language is being used—formatting software will hyphenate foreign languages like they would in English, which is often incorrect.

Much like with paperback and e-book covers, you must also ensure the font you use for your book's interior has the accent marks and appropriate quotation marks available for the manuscript.

If you are formatting Arabic or Asian translations, you may need to have software that will format your text to be read right to left or your paragraphs to run horizontally or vertically in the manuscript. If your translator doesn't format the text for you, you may need to outsource the work to a freelancer who has software that can accommodate these languages. It's also a good idea to have a native speaker or two proofread your interior file in order to catch any errors you wouldn't know exist.

WRAPPING IT UP WITH A PRETTY BOW

There is no one-size-fits all answer to the questions of how to decide on a cover change for your translated book. It's a good idea to spend a little time researching not only your sales data but also the data of similar books in your genre in that country. Reach out to your readers who may natively speak the language as well to help decide what is best for your business. ∎

Grace Snoke

Grace Snoke

Grace Snoke is a 42-year-old author and personal assistant residing in Lincoln, Nebraska. Having been a corporate journalist for more than a decade and a video game journalist for even longer, writing has been something she has always enjoyed doing. In addition to non-fiction books, she is currently working on a paranormal romance series, and two urban fantasy series under her real name. She has also released more than a dozen illustrated children's books and several non-fiction books. She has been publishing erotica under a pen name since 2017. For more information about her personal assistant business visit: https://spiderwebzdesign.net. Her author site is: https://gracesnoke.com.

YOUR ONE-STOP RESOURCE

INDIE AUTHOR TOOLS

INDIEAUTHORTOOLS.COM

📚 Over 45+ categories of resources, from AI to website builders, all designed to supercharge your self-publishing journey.

✍️ Authentic reviews and real-world case studies from authors who've used these tools to bring their creative visions to life.

👤 A community-powered project, crowdsourced by authors who know exactly what you need because they've been there too!

🚀 Boost your authorial prowess with our popular weekly newsletter, packed with tips, tricks, and updates on the latest tools.

The Language of Marketing Translations

The independent publishing market is known for its ability to adapt to the market quickly, implementing the advice of various author circles to feed an audience of readers. Regardless of publishing strategy or medium, or how you prefer to market, publishing tactics and strategies are endlessly available.

But what if the market is a foreign market? Is marketing a translation different from marketing the original book? And how do you know if you'll have an audience in another language to sell your translation to? In this article, *IAM* explores some ready-to-implement techniques and proven methods for approaching new foreign markets to sell your books.

YOUR AUDIENCE MAY BE WAITING

Determining whether an audience is waiting for you is the easiest way to decide how well the market might bear a translation of your books. Consider the first place you might find your readers: your network. This means looking in places where they hang out and asking them if there is a specific language they would like to see one of your books translated into. Facebook Pages, Groups, and your author newsletter are great places to poll an audience who is already used to seeing your name. Although this is not an exact judge of how many readers are in a potential market, it gives you an indication of how well your book might sell in a foreign market upon release. Furthermore, recruiting those who are already looking for your book in a foreign language can create advocates for your book within that network, building the buzz for its release.

Amazon itself is also a wealth of information, able to show you your sales performance across all Amazon storefronts, such as Germany, Canada, Mexico, and more, through a single dashboard, through which you can filter results by country. To check how well your book might do in a foreign market against comparative titles, switch to the

Amazon page for the language you wish to research and start searching for books in your genre using category searches and keyword searches. Then look at the books' rankings on that market's Amazon store to know how well a particular book is selling.

Pro Tip: Enter a book's ranking information into a calculator such as Kindlepreneur's free Amazon sales calculator to estimate the total sales of that book per day.

PAID ADVERTISING

Getting your book into readers' hands is the easy part. Convincing them they should choose your book among thousands of choices can be much harder. Paid advertising, specifically pay-per-click advertising, is a staple of most indie author businesses, and applying pay-per-click strategies to foreign markets is as simple as creating campaigns that target the foreign market. For example, Amazon allows a user to access its ads platform for each Amazon market.

The setup is the same as the US market, but you will need your translated books on the Amazon market first. Then you will need ad copy to go with the ad and keywords in the foreign language.

Pro Tip: Negotiate this with the translator ahead of time. Provide them with a document of translated ad copy, phrases, and keywords that you've seen success with in the past to save from having to ask for it later.

Another option for paid ads platforms is using Facebook's detailed targeting ad campaigns to specifically target markets outside the US. A lot of the same suggestions for setting up Amazon ads in foreign countries apply here as well. Use ad copy in your target language and select your target country as the location to display the ad. You will need to input your translated ad copy, the correct images, and the correct storefront to send readers to. If you're sending traffic to Amazon, you need to select the store in which your translated book is listed.

CONSIDERATIONS

A common question is "Will my current marketing strategies work as effectively for a translation's audience?" The answer isn't a simple yes or no; instead, it depends on how well you know your audience and what they are looking for in a story. When you run high-performing ads to a translation's audience, you risk losing nuance in the text, tropes, and understanding of the story based on the ad and ad copy. To combat this potential pitfall, authors can rely on their translator to provide equivalent copy, then use vigorous testing as they would for the primary market. While it would be great to simply implement high-performing ads again, it is better to use them as a starting point for testing new iterations.

SOCIAL MEDIA

Social media platforms outside of the paid advertising portions are the digital town square, and readers tend to be online and in circles they can relate to. Consider looking online for Facebook Groups or Pages dedicated to translated books for those who are looking to read stories in their native tongue. Be sure to check the posting rules of the Group before you start.

Pro Tip: Search within social media groups for questions related to translations and other genre-specific keywords to find readers who are looking for books in a specific language. Then, look at the answers people provide on where to locate those books. This can be a valuable tool not to hawk your books but rather to find new places to engage with a community of readers who want books in other languages.

CONTENT MARKETING

Similar to social media usage, content marketing on social channels such as Facebook, Instagram, and TikTok is the process in which a user creates

posts, videos, and copy to engage an audience or to build one if they don't already have followers. Social media channels run on algorithms that excel at showing your content to people it determines will engage with it. Consider a holistic social media campaign centered on your translated text, reviews, translated covers, and more to help find new readers of foreign languages. Authors should ensure first that their target audience for the translation can be found on the social media platforms they're using, as some countries cannot access certain sites; then, they need to be sure the platform they are using to try to reach readers is popular among their audience within that country. It's not worth the effort to market your books on one site if all your potential readers prefer to use another.

EMAIL LIST BUILDING

Sometimes, advertising your book after it is live on retailers isn't your only strategy. Authors may choose to build their readership before a book is even released by collecting email addresses from readers. Authors familiar with the term "reader magnet" might already know how this works. This exchange normally takes place using a loss leader, or something of value such as a sample chapter, novel, or short story, given away in exchange for a reader's email address and permission to send them emails.

Building an email list in advance of a translated book's release would also require you to translate your reader magnet into a foreign language, then to use Facebook ads and other platforms to advertise where readers can download the translated magnet in exchange for their email address. Keep in mind this may also require the messaging within the emails communicating with the reader to be translated.

As with your primary market, collaborating with another author in your genre who is already established in a foreign market is a great way to feed their audience with more of what they're looking for while giving your book visibility. Reach out to

other authors about swapping newsletter shout-outs in your translated language, arrange social media posts, and otherwise work collaboratively to share the news that your translated books are ready for others to enjoy.

Like any move you make in your indie author business, consider all outcomes and your expectations on how any decision may affect things moving forward. Investing in the creation and marketing of a translation has a lot in common with a traditional book launch, and authors who are looking to leap into translations need to be ready to answer the question of "Now, how do I get my book out to readers?" ■

David Viergutz

David Viergutz

David Viergutz is a disabled Army Veteran, Law Enforcement Veteran, husband and proud father. He is an author of stories from every flavor of horror and dark fiction. One day, David's wife sat him down and gave him the confidence to start putting his imagination on paper. From then on out his creativity has no longer been stifled by self-doubt and he continues to write with a smile on his face in a dark, candle-lit room.

Très Chic International Typefaces for Your Next Translation

When writing and publishing, the goal for most authors isn't to toss words onto the page, then sit back and wait for someone to pay for the privilege of reading their literary brilliance. A lot of hard work goes into getting all the pieces of the book production process just right in the hope of converting readers to fans.

That's why style matters. Tropes aren't the only expectation readers have when it comes to genre; they also have style expectations for things like body text and book cover or title fonts. And whether it's the classic elegance of serif fonts or the modern simplicity of sans serif, choosing the right font can significantly impact readability and overall aesthetic appeal. For body text, serif fonts like Times New Roman or Garamond are commonly preferred for their readability in print and the way the serifs guide the reader's eyes along the text. Sans serif fonts like Arial or Helvetica, on the other hand, are popular in digital formats because of their clean and modern appearance.

Beyond aesthetics and readability, however, when planning for translations, authors and designers need to consider the linguistic nuances of different languages. Certain characters, such as ü, ñ, or é, may be integral to conveying meaning accurately in translated works. Choosing fonts with comprehensive language support ensures that all text, including special characters, remains clear and legible across different language editions.

While it's always a good idea for an author to exercise a certain level of creative control over their end product, approaching a translation project by working with a designer can provide access to a wider array of tools and licensed fonts, resulting in significant cost and time savings. Although companies like Google Fonts offer all their fonts as free, open-source tools, and have even started to integrate into formatting platforms like Atticus, many companies who offer specialized fonts require the purchase of a commercial license if a user wishes to produce content to be sold.

When choosing a font, another important point to consider is how the reader will consume the content. While monospaced fonts like Courier or Menlo work well with print formats, they are designed to maintain a consistent amount of space between characters and don't resize well on most mobile and e-reading devices or applications. Reflowable fonts such as Georgia are better suited for e-book formats like EPUB because they allow the reader to customize things like font size and line spacing based on screen size and personal preference.

Whether you're working with a designer or selecting fonts for your book yourself, for those seeking accessible and budget-friendly font solutions, several tools offer a diverse range of typefaces to suit every project.

- https://thebookdesigner.com/book-font-guide is a site that covers everything an author needs to know about font selection.
- https://dafont.com allows users to download various free fonts in English and several international languages. Downloads are available for either Windows or Mac operating systems.
- https://myfonts.com is a subscription site but allows free access to a fantastic knowledge base. Click on the arrow next to the Learn option in the top menu bar to display a dropdown menu of free content.
- https://fontjoy.com is a free, AI-based tool that guides authors in pairing fonts that work well together across the various design elements within a book.

Additionally, here are five free fonts suitable for a range of genres and international languages. The fonts listed below would work well as either titles or interior typefaces in your books.

Montserrat

Type: Geometric sans serif

Use: Book covers or body text

Genres: Contemporary Fiction, Young Adult, Non-Fiction

Languages: Latin script languages, including English, Spanish, French, and German

Cost: Free for personal and commercial use

Source: Google Fonts (https://fonts.google.com/specimen/Montserrat)

Montserrat is a versatile and modern font with a geometric aesthetic. Its clean lines and wide range of weights make it suitable for various genres and design styles. Montserrat offers extensive language support, making it an excellent choice for authors with international audiences.

Minion Pro

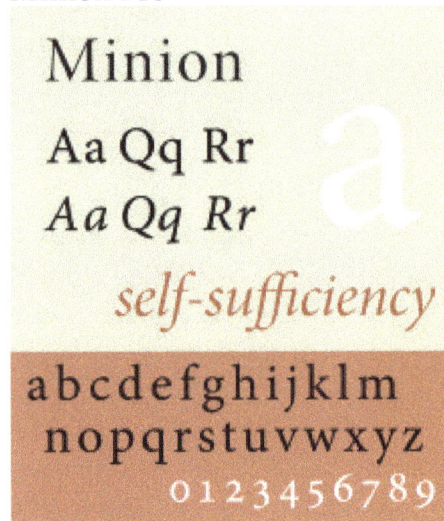

Type: Serif

Use: Book covers, book titles, and body text

Genres: Historical Fiction, Mystery, Romance

Languages: Supports Latin script languages, including Vietnamese, as well as Greek, Armenian, and Cyrillic alphabets

Cost: Free for personal use; commercial licensing available for $569 through Adobe Fonts subscription (https://fontspring.com/fonts/adobe/minion-pro)

Source: Adobe Original

Minion Pro is available in sixty-four styles encompassing a variety of weights, widths, and sizes. It sports a clean, neutral look that lends itself to a variety of uses.

Jenn Mitchell

Jenn Mitchell writes Urban Fantasy and Weird West, as well as culinary cozy mysteries under the pen name, J Lee Mitchell. She writes, cooks, and gardens in the heart of South Central Pennsylvania's Amish Country. When she's not doing these things, she dreams of training llama riding ninjas.

She enjoys traveling, quilting, hoarding cookbooks, Sanntangling, and spending time with the World's most patient and loving significant other.

Roboto

Roboto
Aa Ee Rr
Aa Ee Rr a
Confectionery
abcdefghijklm
nopqrstuvwxyz
0123456789

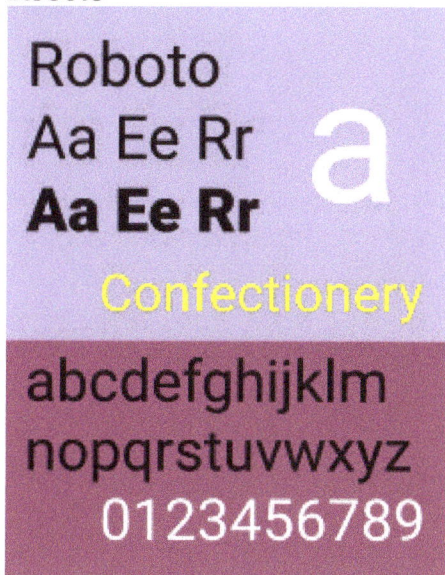

Type: Sans serif

Use: On-screen text for e-books, newsletters, or websites

Genres: Science Fiction, Thriller, Self-Help

Languages: Supports Latin script languages, as well as Greek and Cyrillic alphabets

Cost: Free for personal and commercial use

Source: Google Fonts (https://fonts.google.com/specimen/Roboto)

Roboto is a modern and versatile sans serif font developed by Google for its operating system. Its balanced proportions and clear letterforms make it suitable for a wide range of genres and design applications. Roboto ensures consistent readability across diverse language families.

Libre Baskerville

Type: Serif

Genres: Literary Fiction, Poetry, Biography

Use: Body text

Languages: Supports Latin script languages with extended character sets

Cost: Free for personal and commercial use

Source: Google Fonts (https://fonts.google.com/specimen/Libre+Baskerville)

Libre Baskerville is a modern interpretation of the classic Baskerville typeface. Its generous x-height and open counters enhance readability, making it an excellent choice for long-form text. It offers extensive language support for multilingual projects.

Nunito

Type: Sans serif

Use: Body text and display copy

Genres: Children's books, graphic novels, travel guides

Languages: Supports Latin script languages and Vietnamese

Cost: Free for personal and commercial use

Source: Google Fonts (https://fonts.google.com/specimen/Nunito)

Nunito is a friendly and versatile sans serif font designed for optimal legibility across various platforms. Its rounded letterforms and generous spacing make it particularly suitable for children's books and visually engaging content.

Choosing the right fonts for book design is a crucial factor in positioning yourself for success. By considering factors like readability, language support, and aesthetic appeal, authors can create visually captivating and accessible works that resonate with readers worldwide. With the plethora of free and commercially licensed font options available, authors now have the tools they need to bring their literary visions to life in print and digital formats for markets the world over. ■

Jenn Mitchell

BOOK REPORT
Goes Wide

The Toronto Indie Author Conference in early May saw a new face in the indie author world. But though Toronto was his first conference, Liam Gray is not new to publishing. And the branded T-shirt he wore signified he'd been around for a while, as many recognized the iconic colorful circle logo of his company, Book Report.

Book Report, a book sales analytics tool that touts itself as a "simple and powerful" live sales dashboard, has been used by indie authors for years, but until recently, it was limited to one platform: Amazon.

No longer is that the case. Gray, a self-taught software developer, has cracked the code to enable authors to add not just their KDP reports but also their sales reports from wide platforms such as Kobo, Barnes & Noble, and Draft2Digital, with more being added each week. While these features are reliable and available to anyone, they're currently in "public beta" and will remain so for another couple of months.

When asked why he first created the program, a browser extension that links to your publishing accounts and displays the data in a clear and pleasing format, Gray said he made it for himself. In 2014, when he first graduated high school, in an effort to earn money, he published a series of novels under a pen name. But he quickly found the native tools on Amazon's Kindle Direct Publishing dashboard to be limited. Deciding he could make something better, he put his fledgling coding skills to work. And he was kind enough to share his creation with his author friends.

One of the first additions to his project was a request from his friends on K-Boards and remains a user favorite to this day: an optional cha-ching that sounds every time a new sale is registered.

"It wasn't a day 1 feature, but it was a day 2 feature," Gray says with a chuckle.

Since then, he's been working hard to improve his skills, creating new features, updating the code, and now, adding additional retailers. It's a pain point many authors have asked to solve, and he's happy to finally be able to offer a solution. One other feature he's committed to offering is a free tier. Book Report costs just $19 per month, but only for authors earning $1,000 per month or more. For anyone earning less than that, you can access all the features—including that "cha-ching" sound—for free.

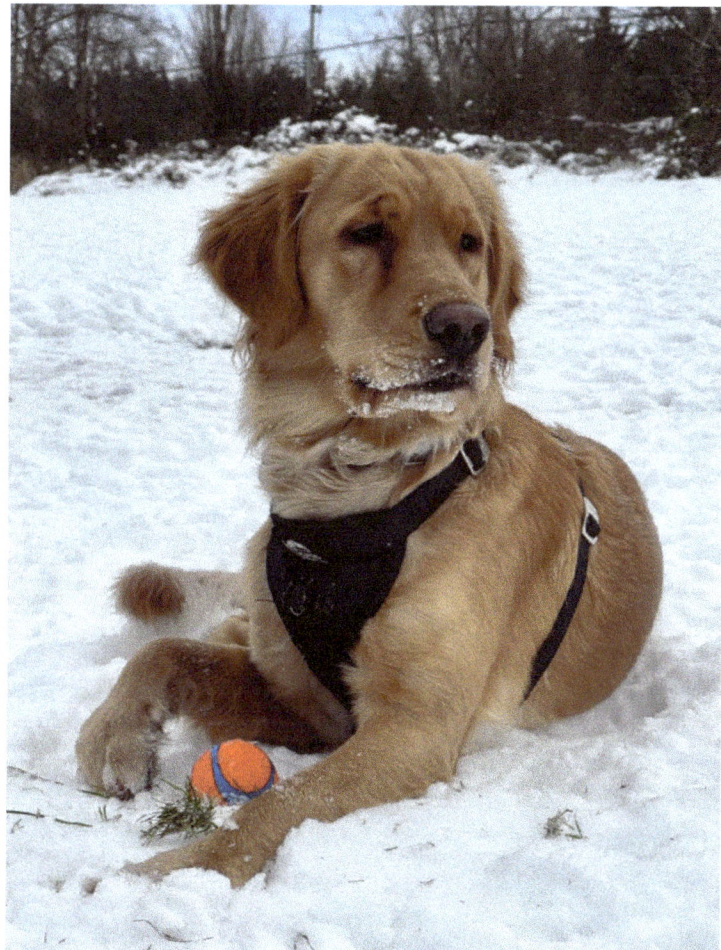

Most people would be surprised to learn that Book Report is not a big company; it's just Gray and his golden retriever, Molly. At one point in time, he outsourced the customer service, but no longer. Pointing to his smart watch, Gray jokes that every time someone emails, his wrist buzzes. Yes, it can be distracting, but he says, "I want to stay connected and gather the feedback directly from the authors."

In addition to Kindle Direct Publishing, the complete list of distribution platforms currently compatible with Book Report through the open beta includes Draft2Digital, Google Play Books, Kobo Writing Life, Barnes & Noble Press, ACX, Apple Books, Findaway Voices, IngramSpark, and Smashwords via Draft2Digital. Learn more about how Book Report integrates with these retailers and watch for updates at https://support.getbookreport.com/hc/en-us. ■

Robyn Sarty

Robyn Sarty

Robyn Sarty is the author of two novels and several short stories and manages her own publishing company. She loves helping other authors with their books and can often be found nerding out over story elements with her friends. She spent five years as a project coordinator for an international engineering firm and now uses those skills to chase writers instead of engineers and hopes it will be good training for her first marathon. Growing up as a third culture kid, books were the one constant in her life, and as such, Robyn believes that books are portals to the magic that lies within, and authors are wielders of that magic. She also admits to being a staunch, loyal, and unabashed supporter of the Oxford comma.

From the Stacks

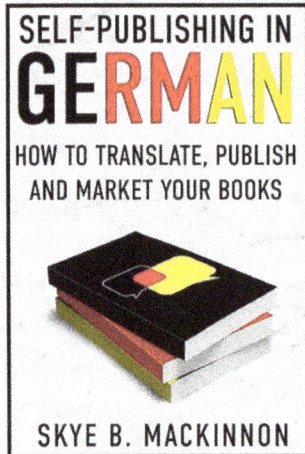

Self-Publishing in German: How to Translate, Publish and Market Your Books
https://books2read.com/u/mB2q7v
The German market is one of the fastest growing markets in publishing today, and the options for translating your books from one language to another continue to grow. *Self-Publishing in German* by Skye B. MacKinnon promises to teach you what to look for in a translator and what to be wary of. This guide on German translation contains insider tips, expert advice, and case-study analyses from other authors, all in support of getting your book translated and taking advantage of a growing market.

Rev Voice Recorder
https://www.rev.com/apps-and-tools/voice-recorder
A free voice recording app available to both iPhone and Android users, Rev Voice Recorder is a two-in-one audio recorder and simple transcription tool that can help authors transition into dictation without the need for additional tools or provide an easy way to add to your word count while away from your writing desk. The app is easy to use and can generate a transcript in under five minutes with 90 percent accuracy, according to its website, and offers both human and AI transcription services.

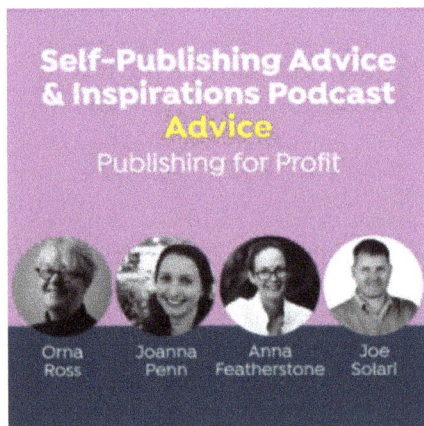

The Self-Publishing Advice Podcast
https://selfpublishingadvice.org/podcast
The Alliance of Independent Authors's podcast, *AskALLi*, is hosted by seasoned authors and ALLi members Orna Ross and Joanna Penn. On the show, they share advanced publishing techniques for seasoned authors and cover how to create better books, find new readers, and operate a successful indie author business. ALLi is a global membership non-profit organization promoting excellence in self-publishing.

When Word for Word Doesn't Work

NAVIGATING THE INTRICACIES OF TRANSLATING YOUR BOOKS INTO A FOREIGN LANGUAGE

As writers, we choose our words and phrases carefully. Sometimes we agonize over them. Whether it's coming up with a title for a book, a character using slang and idioms you're familiar with, or a turn of phrase used in describing a scene, you picked those words for a reason.

However, when translating your book into other languages, you quickly learn that some phrases don't make sense. An English idiom may not carry over to another language and would leave the readers confused, or perhaps a direct translation of your book's single-word title has a different, perhaps even negative, connotation in that language.

So what do you do when your choice of words does not work? Although there is no one right answer, we can provide some options to consider.

Pro Tip: Even though this article talks about going from English to another language, these same issues can occur when going from your native language to English or another language. Even marketing copy can get lost in translation, so it never hurts to take extra care with your words when you're working across languages.

BOOK TITLES OR SERIES NAMES

As authors, we spend hours coming up with the perfect series name and book title for our books. Even if that name has been used a half dozen times or more, it can be used over and over in English-speaking countries. But in other countries, like Germany, book titles that are translated into German cannot have been used before. Nobody else can use a title identical to another, and prior to publishing, you or your translator must research to make sure the title you've chosen doesn't exist.

In other cases, some phrases used in English for a book title might not translate correctly into another language, or they may have negative connotations.

Before fretting over this too much, it is a good idea to discuss any potential issues with your translator. You might already have alternate book titles and series names in mind that you can suggest as options, but in some languages and genres, it may be common enough to continue using an English title and then add a line on the cover specifying that it's been translated to a specific language. You may also ask your translator to suggest a title based on their knowledge of your book and the language. If you used an idiom for a book title or series name, there may be an equivalent saying in the new language that will work. There doesn't seem to be an issue with marketability when changing a book title or series name into a foreign language, so stay flexible, and don't fret.

IDIOMS

Different languages, and even different dialects of the same language, have unique phrases that carry specific meaning beyond the literal. What makes perfect sense in Australia may not make sense to someone from the United States. This is even more true when translating to another language.

Since we speak the language every day and use idioms without much thought, we don't realize that others who speak other languages natively may not understand specific phrases or uses of a word. Before translating your book, you might ask your street team, or readers, to let you know of idioms you use regularly so you can provide a list and definitions for your translator.

Alternatively, you can ask your translator to check with you about any confusing phrases in the book so you can provide an explanation. They may have a similar expression in their language and be able to tell you what it directly translates to in English, as well as what it means.

UNIQUE WORDS OR PHRASES

Fantasy, High Fantasy, LitRPG, GameLit, and Science Fiction often have unique names, words, or phrases used for spells, spell names, money, races, or far-future scientific terms. If you're translating these books, you may wish to create a list of these terms and phrases and identify whether they are a unique language you created or based on an existing language, like Latin. You may decide you want the original language for those to remain the same. However, if there are some that you wouldn't mind having changed for a better reader experience, you may provide the phrases used and an explanation for what they mean, and let your translator know you're okay with those being changed.

If you have a world bible for your series, it may be helpful to share it with your translator, so they can refer to it as needed.

A FINAL NOTE

Remember that a translator wants your book to be successful because if it is, they will end up getting more business. If they ask about rewriting something to make it work better in their language, they aren't doing it for the sake of rewriting your story but to make it sound good to their readers.

As important as your words may be, don't sacrifice their impact in a translation. Your stories will sell better when they make sense to your readers—and you can have fun learning phrases unique to other languages in the process.

WANT MORE INFORMATION?

Check out the articles and resources below for more information on the translation process and tips for making it run smoothly.

- Kindlepreneur, "How to Get a Book Translated" (https://kindlepreneur.com/book-translation)
- IBPA PubSpot, " Lost in Translation: How to Get a Book Translated from English into a Foreign Language" (https://pubspot.ibpa-online.org/article/lost-in-translation)
- Ulatus professional translation services, "The Art of Translating Books: Unlocking New Worlds for Readers Everywhere" (Visit https://ulatus.com/translation-blog)
- Writing Tips Oasis craft blog, "5 Tips for Getting Your Books Translated into Different Languages" (Visit https://writing-tipsoasis.com)
- Scribe Media, "How To Translate Your Book (& Reach International Markets)" (https://scribemedia.com/translating-books)
- VeraContent translation services, "How to translate a book: Everything you need to know" (Visit https://veracontent.com)
- 20Books Vegas hosted several panels on navigating translations as an indie author. Visit https://youtube.com/@20Booksto50kRLiveEvents and search "translations" to watch sessions from previous years' conferences.

Grace Snoke

Grace Snoke

Grace Snoke is a 42-year-old author and personal assistant residing in Lincoln, Nebraska. Having been a corporate journalist for more than a decade and a video game journalist for even longer, writing has been something she has always enjoyed doing. In addition to non-fiction books, she is currently working on a paranormal romance series, and two urban fantasy series under her real name. She has also released more than a dozen illustrated children's books and several non-fiction books. She has been publishing erotica under a pen name since 2017. For more information about her personal assistant business visit: https://spiderwebzdesign.net. Her author site is: https://gracesnoke.com.

From Waves to Words

TOOLS FOR WRITING BY THE SEA

Welcome to Newport Beach, a coastal gem nestled in Southern California. Its allure is undeniable, beckoning travelers with its glistening shores and cerulean waves. Spanning over ten miles along the public park system, the Balboa Peninsula showcases the beauty of the California coast. It's a place where a writer could seek solace, drawn by the rhythmic crashing of waves and the whisper of the sea breeze.

This is one of my favorite locations to write in the spring and early summer. Beach writing gives you a break from being inside, both at home and in the local coffeehouse. It can offer a popular respite for authors looking to change up their scenery during warmer months or searching for an escape from distractions or other responsibilities in order to focus on their creative flow.

For the solitary writer venturing to any beach, preparation is key to a successful writing session. Here's a list of essential tools to bring along.

Notebook or journal: First and foremost, you'll need your trusty companion for capturing thoughts, ideas, and observations amid the tranquil surroundings.

A surface to write on: I use a rubberized laptop board, but anything sturdy that fits on your lap and is waterproof will work.

Pens: Whether it's a fountain pen, ballpoint pen, or gel pen, ensure you have writing utensils at the ready. Fountain pens are a choice, but they can be susceptible to sand damage. Use these at your own risk.

Tablet or phone with a protective water sleeve (optional): For those who prefer digital writing tools, a tablet and phone can offer convenience and versatility. I use dictation through an app on my phone at the beach instead of a keyboard. I recommend leaving your laptop at home. The wind picks up plenty of sand, and this could damage your laptop's keyboard.

Pro Tip: Although recorders can be helpful when dictating in an indoor writing space, it may not be necessary for your beach outing. Phones are typically responsive enough to work effectively, and certain apps include AI to add in punctuation as you speak.

Apps for beach writing: If you prefer dictation, several apps allow you to record on your phone or tablet. You can access Google Docs, Otter, and Jotter even with a waterproof sleeve on your device. Upload your words to the cloud, and your work will be waiting for you once you get home, ready for revision. If you still want to type, you can access your phone keyboard through the sleeve. Google Docs and Jotter both have screen access, and a host

of writing programs such as Scrivener (Apple only), MS Word, and Pages have apps as well.

Water bottle: Hydration is paramount, especially under the warm summer sun. A large water bottle ensures you stay refreshed and focused throughout your writing session.

Sunscreen: Be mindful of sun exposure. It is easy to lose track of time on the beach. Aim for a sunscreen with an SPF of 30 or higher, according to the American Academy of Dermatology, and reapply every two hours for the best coverage.

Beach umbrella or personal sun shelter: I swear by my umbrella at the beach, but I find a sun shelter not only blocks the sun but also provides wind protection for my notebooks and fountain pens.

Beach bags or a small wagon: Getting stuff to your spot from a car can be difficult. Find a means to pack all your gear for easy transport.

Equipped with these essentials, a writer can seek the perfect sunny spot to unleash their creativity. In the solitude of a Newport Beach morning, I find my sanctuary—a place where words flow and inspiration knows no bounds. You may find the same at your local beach this summer. ◾

Wendy Van Camp

Wendy Van Camp

Wendy Van Camp is the Poet Laureate for the City of Anaheim, California. Her work is influenced by cutting edge technology, astronomy, and daydreams. A graduate of the Ad Astra Speculative Fiction Workshop, Wendy is a nominated finalist for the Elgin Award, for the Pushcart Prize, and for a Dwarf Stars Award. Her poems, stories, and articles have appeared in: "Starlight Scifaiku Review", "The Junction", "Quantum Visions", and other literary journals. She is the poet and illustrator of "The Planets: a scifaiku poetry collection" and editor of the annual anthology "Eccentric Orbits: An Anthology of Science Fiction Poetry". Find her at https://wendyvancamp.com

The Fourth Inflection Point

THE AUTHOR WHEEL CO-FOUNDER MEGAN HASKELL MAPS OUT THE MANY PATHS OF INDIE PUBLISHING

The road to indie authorship has changed drastically since it became an option for story-tellers looking to make a living with their words. From on-demand printing to crowd-funding special editions, the rise of e-readers to generative AI tools for drafting and marketing, the publishing landscape has evolved rapidly from where it started—and authors today have more options than ever for how to manage their business. In the first of a five-part series, The Author Wheel co-founder Megan Haskell explains where the industry is headed by considering where it's been—and what the many paths of indie publishing may mean for your career.

It's often said that history is the best teacher. Reflecting on how indie publishing developed can help us anticipate the changes yet to come. In knowing our options, past and present, we can carve our own personal path to success.

Looking at the future of our industry, there are countless new opportunities on the horizon. From direct sales to subscription models and transmedia opportunities, authors are forging their own paths to success based on their personal motivations, skills, and long-term goals. Embracing the craft of story-telling while focusing on human experience, they are finding their niche, and readers love them for it.

But to understand where we are going, it's important to understand where we've been—and what makes this shift different from others we've faced before. As we stand on the precipice of change, let's take a moment to look at our roots.

TRADITIONAL PUBLISHING

From the advent of the printing press until the late twentieth century, publishers controlled the market. They had the means and the money to print books and get them into bookstores. It was a rare author who could be successful without following the traditional path of finding an agent who would pitch publishers and, hopefully, secure a contract.

Three major inflection points changed the industry and created the self-publishing landscape we know today.

THE FIRST INFLECTION POINT: PRINT-ON-DEMAND (POD)

In the 1980s and '90s, new technology arose that could print one book at a time at a relatively low cost. Self-published authors no longer needed to pay thousands of dollars for a print run that may or may not sell nor store thousands of books in their garage.

The challenge lay in getting self-published titles into readers' hands. Even with the internet on the rise, the infrastructure didn't yet exist to facilitate online book sales efficiently. Printing had become easier, but distribution remained difficult.

THE SECOND INFLECTION POINT: AMAZON'S KINDLE DEVICE AND PUBLISHING PLATFORM

On November 19, 2007, Amazon released the first Kindle e-reader. Readers could store hundreds, even thousands, of books on a machine that was smaller than a regular paperback. It sold out in five and a half hours. Amazon spent five months trying to catch up with demand.

At the same time, Amazon launched Kindle Direct Publishing (KDP), which allowed authors to upload their digital books to the Kindle store for sale. With POD integrated into the system, indie authors now had a platform to distribute books to readers.

With KDP and POD, there were no up-front costs to publish, no warehouse or storage fees, and essentially no barriers to entry. Anybody could publish a book with a few clicks of their mouse. By 2010, independent authors were finding incredible financial success with e-books. It was a gold rush, and the faster you wrote and published, the more money you'd make.

THE THIRD INFLECTION POINT: A MATURING MARKET

The Kindle proved there was a market for readers who wanted the convenience of a digital library. KDP proved authors were ready, willing, and able to meet reader demands. Other e-book platforms and devices soon followed.

The market grew crowded.

Reaching readers had become easy. Catching their attention had become hard. Modern-day indie authors not only had to produce quality stories quickly; they had to invest in professional covers and copyediting as well. They became experts at writing book descriptions and ad copy to complement their full-length novels. They acted as their own small press, or they failed.

THE DAWN OF A NEW AGE

The rapid release model combined with increased marketing demands had a downside: author burnout. Once-prolific writers found themselves unable to maintain the fast pace. A desire to slow down, do less, but do it better began rising through the ranks.

Then came AI. Using Language Learning Models (LLMs) and visual AI programs, some authors have been able to increase their writing speed or decrease time spent on marketing. Others stepped away from the rapid release model to connect with readers between book launches with expanded story worlds, subscriptions, or transmedia projects. Still others have moved into direct sales by managing their own online storefronts, offering readers exclusive products and experiences not available on the traditional retail platforms.

We now face a fourth inflection point.

For authors entering the market today, there's no longer a single path to publication. There's no "right way" to become an author. It's complex and confusing, but with change comes opportunity.

Welcome to the new indie author age. ■

Megan Haskell

Megan Haskell

Megan Haskell pens tales of myth, magic, and mayhem featuring strong female heroines and monsters of every size. She's the award-winning author of The Sanyare Chronicles fantasy adventure and The Rise of Lilith contemporary fantasy series, and co-founder of The Author Wheel Podcast and courses for writers. With more than fifteen years of writing and publishing experience, her goal is to help you Clarify, Simplify, and Implement your own best path to an author career. Find out more at www.MeganHaskell.com or www.AuthorWheel.com.

CLONE YOURSELF

Custom Chat GPT Bots

Harnessing AI's knowledge base and expand your skills and expertise in vital areas such as:

Life and Business Coaching
Mastering Marketing and Newsletter Strategies
Crafting Captivating Blurbs and Social Posts
Enhancing Time Management
Elevating Customer Service
Writing Compelling Ad, Product, and Landing Page Copy

And that's just the beginning.

INDIEAUTHORTRAINING.COM

www.ingramcontent.com/pod-product-compliance
Lightning Source LLC
Chambersburg PA
CBHW042342030426
42335CB00030B/3431